The Music of this Ruin

A collection of poetry by

Patricia Barone

Margaret Hasse, copy editing

ISBN: 978-81-8253-724-8
First Edition: 2021
Rs. 200/-

Cyberwit.net
HIG 45 Kaushambi Kunj, Kalindipuram
Allahabad - 211011 (U.P.) India
http://www.cyberwit.net
Tel: +(91) 9415091004
E-mail: info@cyberwit.net

Printed at Repro India Limited.

For my children, Matt Barone and Claire Barone, with much love.

In memory of my grandmother, Elizabeth Cuthbert Ryan, who showed me how to persevere through the final stage of life and find joy.

In gratitude for my R.N. nursing education at Anoka-Ramsey Community College.

My heartfelt thanks to the nurses who have heroically worked through the pandemic.

Acknowledgements

Some of the poems in this manuscript received a Loft-McKnight Award of Distinction in Poetry, chosen by Marilyn Hacker. They were published in *Things That Fall From the Sky*, 1994, The Loft Inc., in a limited edition:

"Avonelle Wanders in the Dining Room"

"Now That All Your Questions Have One Answer"

"Crying"

"From the Open Window, Her Song,"

"Through This Permeable Shell"

"The Mourning Dove"

"He Used to Kiss My Feet"

"You Have to Hand It to Her"

"The Eagle"

"My Father Contemplates His Days"

is also in Broad Wings, Long Legs: A Rookery of Heron Poems, 2021; editor James S. Rogers

"The Glorified Body," Commonweal

"Schatzie's Party," Sidewalks

"The Buzzards," Sidewalks

"Dividing the Dark Into Parcels," and

"Gift", *The Talking of Hands*, New Rivers Press

“Robert and Mike, a Love Story” and

“Melvin and Mary, Another Love Story,” in press

Wising Up Press anthology, *Flip Side*, 2021

“Last Night on a Northern Lake,” *To Sing Along the Way*, New Rivers Press

“Amazing Grace,” in *War Poetry,* Winning Writers, 2007

“From Her Own Mind,” *Tiltawhirl* (*Umbrella Journal*)

“Waiting in the Night With Mary, *The Shop,* Ireland

“Genius at Home in the Universe,” in *Inspired by Tagore,* published by Sampad,

South Asian Arts, and British Council, Birmingham, UK, 2012.

“I Got the Bone Loss Blues,” and “The Family Recessional Recorded” were also published

in *Your Funny, Funny Face,* Blue Light Press, 2018, by Patricia Barone

CONTENTS

THE AVIARY

Romana's Concert at the Nursing Home

While playing stride piano
in her own jazz band,
her flashy digits drummed the keys, puls*at*ing
the wry and funky off-beats
of her melody.

Romana's strident left hand thrummed
    C minor seventh chords,
as her right-hand flipped
those flatted fifths.

She played with far-out octaves
till she was sixty-five and—side men gone—
ornery joints won't let her hands
leap the keys or syncopate.

No time for grieving—
she took up the flute,
called it her old arm bone.
She tried to blow full tones,
but couldn't sustain her breath
to float the notes,
unlike Sonny Rollins on his sax.
She couldn't even count on old reliable
inhale-exhales, the basic part of any gig.

When her Irish nephew sent her uilleann pipes,
for the life of her, she couldn't
hold the key. Her first notes' wavering

sounded like her wails
during concert nightmares
when she can't lift her arms
or purse her lips to shape the stream of music.

She persists with uilleann pipes—
her slack embouchure doesn't matter.
She presses the stale room air
through the bellows with her elbow—
how swell it feels compelling winds
to rush inside the bag, then out
from a sack of breeze she loosens

when her other elbow swings away
from her creaky ribs.

She releases each zephyr easy
in a melody she fingers on the chanter pipe.
Skirls of bagpipe fill our halls.

From pipes so often used for funerals—
heavy on the baritone drone—
she switches to tenor, tuning
her pipes for celebration.

Swaying from side to side,
Romana improvises counter rhythms,
squeezes a blast and fetches her old licks back.

In rhythm with the pumping of her heart,
she lets the music play her.

Avonelle's Last Questions

My body slides out from under me.
My head rolls back. I would look at the stars

If I could, but the ceiling is too dense.
Why do we live in this box?

Why does snow fall from the fan? And papers—
are they invitations?

Bills? Are they sent from God?
All these people—are they wedding guests?

Is this is a feast, I'll wear my best
dress and dancing shoes—where are they?

Why do we wait in the anteroom—What's that knocking,
knocking? Why don't they come in or we go out?

If you're going to be going—Go.
Don't stand talking in the door's mouth.

Nor beneath its lintel, hide from lightning.
Like being on a train, you're neither here nor there.

Though I played nun in her bed sheets, Mother bore me
the usual way—on a path to the mountain.

Getting stuck in the valley for life, I believe
is my life-sentence, not orbital punishment later.

Mother told me, beware of a fool's purse.
It's rusty by dawn; the bishop's miter by stealth.

Is God ready for my death?
I'm waiting for the blandishment of light.

Avonelle Tells Herself Goodbye

Run home, Avonelle—
dark is almost down.
A lamplighter climbs his ladder,

flaring gas tapers—
I'm tardy!

~

I was the one fetched Da
from Dooley's, him singing
little Avi, Agnus Dei,
you're my only
sunshine.

~

Avonelle, recall
how you crossed the bridge,
bringing beer in a bucket
on ironing day?

Ma drank it,
iced cold.

~

Wait, Avonelle
for the chimney sweep

wearing a top hat
to brush the soot
from stars.

Tell him to take you
out the river way,
his carriage pulled
by dray horse—
in style.

~

Why must he grip
my arm so hard?
gasps Avonelle, it hurts!
Just take my heart and weigh it
on the scale.

See blue creeping
up your ankles,
Avonelle.

After skating,
Ma fixed cocoa.
Warm me!

~

Why must your body know
desiccation? Open
the sluice gates.

Avonelle,
you're tasting salt.

~

Freckles fade
on your face, Avonelle—
the Milky Way speeding
from time.

~

Listen—
your breath,
a whistle in the fog,
a long wind tunnel.

Tonight, Avonelle.

Now That All Your Questions Have One Answer

A Letter to Avonelle

In heaven,
where I trust you landed,
after your last unedited breath:
I hope your collection of questions
wins celestial Jeopardy. I hear your voice,
not querulous but musing: *Where do we go?*

Can you tell me? At the feeder table, you fed
yourself, your palest gray eyes unseeing, fixed
pin-point pupils. Your questions rose and roiled,
wafted on the odor of Brussels sprouts. *Where do we go?*

We, your nurses and nurses' aides, were tired
of trying to answer so we said, you're going
to bed after dinner, Avonelle. *Yes, yes,*
you told us, but *when will I*
discern the final cost?

It's all paid for, Avonelle, we said,
no comfort there.

Now that you no longer
lob questions at our answers, Forgive us.

Four Miles High on the Frozen Lake

Maevis, Gladstone's widow, though he isn't dead,
lives alone, Assisted Living. She converses
with the man he was, his photo '53, Life Magazine.

Her dinner on a tray, she doesn't dine with widows
whose husbands, Winnebagos, died in Arizona.
"Grounded snow-birds." Good old days bring pain.

When he's wheeled to her, the surface of his eyes
seals his drowning like that frozen lake, too calm.
Irises stroke-silvered, does he see her or mountains

in his widened pupils? After climbing the Tetons,
he dreamed of plunging, a peregrine falcon's
beak-first dive past juddered ledges, fleeting sky.

Maeve cries as his brother spoons him Jameson's—
Today marl blue, her Gladstone's eyes fog over.

From the Open Window, Her Song

Gathered in wheelchairs near the captives,
some residents don't speak or hear or see
birds perch on rungs or ersatz trees.

The phoebe's droned conviviality
is only understood by Hazel, whose tongue
stutters like the wren's descending triplets.

Her mouth is a nest of consonants;
the veery slurs on vowels. The nurse places
Mellaril on Hazel's tongue.

Flicking wings no longer etch the glass.
But her uncertain ears still hear their concert—
ticks, rings and shrills—but through this cacophony,

doves coo at her window, the cue to resume
moaning her own comfort, her unending tone.

How She'll Travel Home

Sightless, Annie wants to know—
"By cutter, sleigh or bobsled?
The darned blizzard!"
Her blued eye closes,
her pallid eye blinks.
"My white house is hidden
by this perishing snow.
So lead me through the woods—
Watch for poking branches and the ice!"

Annie's roommates screech.
"What a racket!"
Though I say it's Flo and Hilma,
"It's the crows."

They're quarreling over toast, or Annie's gold
teeth, her house key, or the rings of wet
tracks her chair makes in the drifts,
snow breaking from her wheels in frozen crusts.

Crying

The activities lady discusses flightless birds
while Chloe sobs, *Ma! Ma!* till she's short of breath.

Raining more, forever more—
in bushes, nurses' shoes, the freesia.
Chloe cries *woo woo,* her cheeks slick with water
as salty as rain in the sea.

Humidity shorts the door alarm,
gone off for escaping ghosts—Lars Olsen,
Dead at 92, paces the path to Fellowship Park so quickly
we see only footprints in the flattened grass, his gnarly toes
crushing leaves in the gutters.

"What can we do for Chloe"? the new nurse asks.
"Call for a novel med?" The old hand sniffs.
"She's failed 'em all. She's done with chemicals—
it's not her brain but in her heart, this crying."

Chloe's chin trembles. "Where's Daddy?
Why don't he get me out?"

"Finches foster-parent orphaned nestlings,"
says the sweet bird lady.

Beneath Chloe's lids, surging tears
drop in her open mouth and splash
the pebbles in the large wire cage.

"Red in summer," says the lady,
"in winter they resemble sparrows."
Dun tails glisten with Chloe's tears.

Through This Permeable Shell

At noon indigo buntings sing loudest, all
but the incubating female on grayish eggs,
no bigger than Elsie's fingernail. She sits
in broody silence as her male, iridescent chest
sparkling like sequins, swoops in with seeds.

Distressed warbling—the keeper sweeps the cage.
A broom on Elsie's cataracts, her dulling lenses.
Beneath their mother's breast, the hatchlings raise
stubby wings, their feathers with large quills
like cartoon drawings—her granddaughter laughs.

"Which birdie is yours?" Outside her window, Elsie
hears and feels a rufous towhee's rough, vibrating
trill, *chewiiink*, like *drink your tea*. The towhee's
irises seem green like hers before they blink and fade.

You Have to Hand It to Her

Hilma with her gooseberry eyes: she knows
the warren of units at The Home just isn't—
"Room 109! Room 109! Get me! Now!"—
home, not hers, and she hollers, insistent.

The vet with medicine (Ace Bird Supply) finds
Hilma waiting: "The palm warbler's chirping
like a frog—you better check it!" Reminded by
the drooping Victoria fern of gardening, she dips
her cup to water the caladium, "Angels' wings."

She's determined—"I'll live to be one hundred."
In the aviary's back wall of straw, the nest-
pockets fill with eggs, and fledglings fall
like thistles as she pleads her orders,
"Please, damn keeper—put them back!"

Love, I Do Not Go

Their marriage finally brought them to a room
at the Home, *convalescent*, but their situation
was terminal, Mike knew. Carrie would bellow
for him if he went to men's group, a slow walk
by the staff room, chapel, nurses going around
with med carts. Mike is frowning in this photo.

Carrie—only two years ago—photographed
well. She was *there*, eyes humorous. Below
the 40th anniversary photo, hung in their room
by their daughter, was a snap of the tulip walk
to their house, all gone now. Carrie went around
crying for her sprinkling can. "What a situation!"

Mike told their son, "If only she'd sit and eat
with me, but no. She's thinner pacing by our room
and can't remember where it is." Aides put a photo
of Carrie on her door. Not knowing her face, she rounded
every corner but hers. Her ankle band, if she walked
outside, wailed once then kept on buzzing lower.

Like the moan Carrie made escaping. Mike felt low
over his coffee, scanning the news. The world situation
was bad and getting worse. He was just a room-renter
in the Home, on earth. Her feet were clumsy on her rounds.
He saw how hard she was trying—to restore family photos?
The white-outs of their life together. He could walk.

Stroll away as she disappeared. Get a sub-let, a short walk.
He could visit her prison often. Her face, once round,
would wrinkle into smiles, or would she hunch over, lower
her chin, and go right by him? For peace, he needed to situate
himself as her widower. She'd escaped from fun and photos,
left their history. Easy as she left her mind, their double room.

He refused to stay active with Bingo. "I need my own room,
and a separate life," he told their son. "I've tried to quietly sit
with her, but she can't rest." Beginning his own restless walk,
he passed his kit-made clock. Both hands clapped twelve below
their cork ceiling, when she, smiling like an early photograph,
knew him. "You," she said. "Your smell," her arms around him.

He knew it couldn't last, and holding her around her waist,
he kissed her. As they walked South from their northern room,
an aide took a photo of their happy situation for the children.

He Used to Kiss My Feet

Rita wears a pheasant-wing, cocked
over one eye in the photo, *trés chic.*
She leans into her escort whose khakis,
goggles, aviator's silk and belted jacket
whisper *Casablanca.* "I wore that chiffon
scarf to hold my feathers on my head.
For me, his mistress, how he raced that
Bentley like Billy Hell! Those ring-necks
flew from the macadam—he didn't give a damn!

When he was free, he said, a seamstress would fasten
my veil to a dove's breast. "No! I said, "Let's keep
love sweet and naughty!" The nurse says, "Rita, eat—
oatmeal goes down easy." —"I don't have to."
Rita smiles. "Do anything, dahling, I won't."

My Dog Was Smarter Than I Was

Wilma quilted clouds for Canada geese,
black yarn wings on hazy cotton batting,
not itchy wool for her counterpanes, starry
spirals stretched on the quilting frame.

She hung her worn-out comforters beneath
the skylight rafters of the barn, its eaves
fluttered with swallows' forked and pointy tails.

Long twitters unraveled in the air they filled
with iris colored wings above the sheep,
whose breathing in the winter barn gave shape
to a sort of summer. Wilma was only ten when
she left fourth grade forever, to bring the cattle in.

Coral-breasted swallows soared above her,
as her Sheltie herded cows and calves together.

Edna Defends What is Hers

Withdrawing silver feathers,
Edna's unlucky gray jay
left a hole in the air.
Flown to the oak, it perched
    like a cusp of dirty snow.

While Edna tallied logs at the lumber camp,
her husband skedaddled
after the sawmill tramp. Edna didn't care
why or how but, "*What* did he leave me? Poor.
        With seven kids to feed."

A raucous band of gray jays dove
to snatch tossed scraps of fat and oatmeal.
One churlish bird jabbed his beak in her palm.
"To steal my toast hot, the bread I couldn't waste—
        "Me and seven kids to feed."

Even now, her children grown, Edna has to scuffle.
Old Lily is as mean as those jays and grackles.
Lil darts from the pantry with stolen grub.
She lunges her walker hard—on Edna's ankle.
    Giggling, she rolls over—Edna's feet.

No victim, Edna spits out, "Scram!"
and slaps Lil with the only hand that works.
        "Off my private property!"

Fortune Cookies

overheard in Independent Living

1.

You Will Have a Date With Temptation

It's a sad day when the funny papers
are over, when your lover peels
the last grape and pops it
in his mouth, not yours.
Where's the cake, the party favors?

I used to drawl, *Come up and see me some time,*

in a husky voice like Mae's, but now I crave
chocolate, wine, and painless hands.

2.

Expect the Unexpected

Monday I scratch my lotto ticket
at the Grab'n'Go. I always lose.
On Tuesday I get Chinese,
one egg roll with hot mustard.

Inside the pink pastry
excuse for dessert,

I find this disgusting proposal:
You Will Get Unexpected Kisses.

I tweet: *Enough of your promises already.*
I mean you, your sweet stuff
and the thieving Dream-On Corporation.

With the sort of joints I hang out in,
how do I know this message is from God,
a good kisser, or the masseur of my dreams?

3.

Nature, Time and Patience

are the three best physicians—
Nature strikes my joints;
in Time I'll use a cane,
and I'll be damned
if I spend one moment with Patience,
her endless yarn,
her namby-pamby knitting.

She Wasn't Always Like This

Phoebe's brawny daughter
bought her mother's shoes,
girls size four, twice yearly.

The wheels on Phoebe's chair
became a humming bird's blur,
and she'd brake too late.

Her heels just scraped on by
the mischief she caused going fast—
Oops, Hilma's pitcher
tumbles, floods the floor.

"My busy mother. I remember her broiling
walleye, and once this merganser she'd dipped
in paraffin—a pot on top the campfire—to pluck
the feathers easily. She roast it on a spit.

"Mom said diving loons are better fishers than we are.
It's eat and be eaten! Once early, her pole off the bridge,
Ma slept by a phoebe nest, and her name—Fee-bee!—
woke her, reel clicking, the carp breaking loose down river.

"Remember," I just asked her, "your batter recipe for perch?"
"I had golden curls," she said and tried to nibble my nose—
What next? I told her, "how I miss you!"
She pinched my cheeks and rolled away."

The Buzzards

That Eugene O'Day—
he says he used to "rassle herds"
of North Dakota buffalo
upon a thousand acre ranch.
"Lightning struck the prairie—
quick as electric eels!"

He drove the cattle hard,
"till the customers complained
about tough steaks."
Gene lost his lower legs to diabetes.
"Ate too many Johnny cakes
soaked in black molasses.
Maggie, the cook, flipped stacks for us.

Rolling up our beds,
we broke the camp by daybreak.
Those cattle falling in the high cold air?
We left 'em. Left their bones
as toothpicks for the buzzards."

Now his front wheels are jammed
in hind wheels—Iona's geri chair.
He reverses with his able left hand.

"Saw eagles once, talons down,
rip the hides off calves."

Chair in forward gear,
he sets his face toward the sunroom.

Last Night on a Northern Lake

for an Alzheimer's patient

1.

The loon doesn't laugh when snaring
a mackerel, only when it doesn't catch
the merest minnow. From dives that slide
beneath the lake, it pops up, red eyed
in surprise, slick pinions dripping,
empty beak. The loon's yodeled
prat-call is for Alice, who collects
clues of her former self—morsels, things.

She laughs—*ha ha*—and sinks below
the medicine cart, a useless life raft,
and the P.M. nurse's purview.

2.

The moon's chalky face is the loon's empty plate.
Loon's table is set with blue spruce; white-lace
beaches cup the lake's wind-wrinkled waves.

The loon guffaws *hooo-aaah!* and Alice flusters.
She lifts the silver cellars of salt, Hungarian black
pepper sifting on the oval eggs Loon's hapless hen
cracked while laying. Cross-eyed double yolks look
hard at Alice, who locates her hunger near her heart.

She searches for the cake she'll have to swallow
to be smaller, crawl unscathed into the smallest
closet of her family house, be saved.

3.

Crumbs of the loon's cold dinner are pike eggs
then small fries, swimming from Alice, who wades
the hall to salvage words, but steals the nurse's pen.
Toes aching, she can't stay or leave behind the totems
she takes while wandering, her head lower than her wings.

One ankle has her name-band so she can't escape.
Oh no-ooh, intones Alice, her final solo at the Home,
and she floats free. Ululations rise, the choirs of birds
keening against the ways of change. This lake is turning
into pond, then fen, last land. No loons remaining.
On harsh wind currents—

4.

Her mattress moves out upon the water in the wake
of a loon's high chortle, and so many name brands
that she can't use or place are bobbing in the tow-tide.
Husband, children, grandchildren, standing on the dock
far away. Alice housekeeps the flotsam and jetsam—
keys, sweaters, scraps of paper, bowls and fedoras.

Let things go, let them sink beneath the under wing
coverts and the upper wing cross-striped coverts
and the sleek green lores of the loon, as Alice floats
and covets through her dream—Loon's gleaming
blue-black neck band!

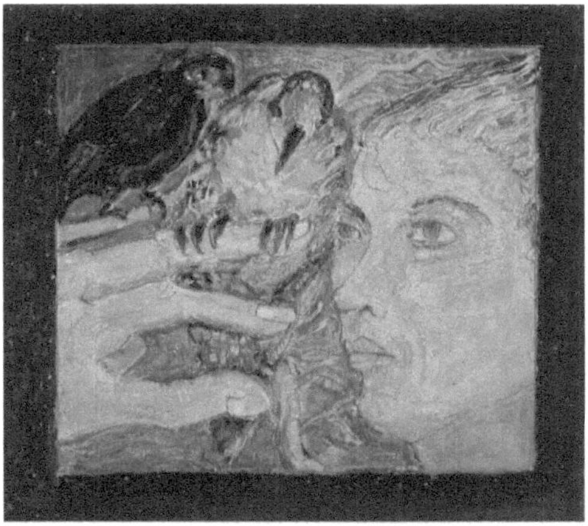

THE LISTENERS

Dividing the Dark into Parcels

The ones who stay awake all night
dividing the dark into parcels,
assigning each
to parts of the body,
input and output:
They write the measurable truth.

The eschar of the wound
in diameter 3.5 centimeters.
The patient is afebrile.

Won't you help me?
Won't you tell me what
to deny. I know
they're keeping me
against my will,
so won't you tell me
what isn't?

The night is divided
into ever more
minute pieces,
each second
has its task.
Each breath,
dry or moist,
its sibilance.

Won't you turn me, won't you
show me the way
home from here, how far
I am so tired.

Each tick of dark
drops through
unsleeping eyes.

The pharmacist's counter ejects
time-release capsules
to dissolve in stomach acid
at the appointed time.

Won't someone help me,
come help me—no, no one
will help me, guess not.

Room after room,
each resident
is lifted gently
or roughly,
from wet pads.
Each sheet is whisked
and rolled beneath
their cheeks.

Want my warm
mother.
Won't my mother
come.

Listening to Their Voices

"In my Father's house are many mansions."

Here below, Agnes steals a hymnal,
Elmer's. He growls and snatches it back.
On her 90th birthday, ruminating over ribbons
she hid from her sisters, Agnes says,
"I don't deserve a cake."

Elmer begs, "A cigarette?"
from the aide, who shrugs.
Evenings lets him use his lighter;
Day shift takes it.
On Nights we can't decide.

Elmer takes his seizure pill with water
thick as pudding, but he chokes,
his throat too sore and swollen.
He roars in organ decibel, *Why!?*

May whoever spins the universe—
let's call her God—listen
to him and all the voices,
broken in sleep.
Elmer pleads for light, not a cigarette.

From a nightmare, Agnes claims her name,
"I'm Mary Agnes Moore"
and place, "I'm in the wrong house."

If I weren't listening,
if I didn't pause my scratching pen,
it would have muffled her voice—

"It wasn't meant to be.
This way. My window's dark,
and I can't see the lake."

From Her Own Mind

Ethrelda dies while floating
from her mind, retired in a home.
The cat gently chews on its sore paw.
A night nurse hustles to punch in.

Rushing out, the P.M. nurse reports
she's late to bed, can't quit, no luck.
She retires her mind in a rented room.
Potato eyes are weeping shoots.

Late in bed, to the shop, from his truck,
the oxygen porter rolls ten tanks.
Potato eyes are weeping shoots.
The kitchen aide jets to Cancun.

The oxygen porter rolls ten tanks.
They sing *Lyda Rose* in the rec. room.
The kitchen aide jets to Cancun.
Sound the alarm for one eloper.

They sing *Lyda Rose* in the rec. room.
Outside, the pond is freezing over.
Sound the alarm for one eloper.
Ethrelda's only lover falls at Anzio.

Out where the pond is freezing over,
worn woman slips in on wet oak leaves.
Ethrelda's only lover falls at Anzio,
shots cracking the ice, ducks, the rushes.

Worn woman slips in on wet oak leaves,
shots cracking the ice, ducks, the rushes.
The cat gently chews on its sore paw.
Ethrelda dies while floating home.

Celia's Attendant Spirits

"Celia's drowning in her own fluids,"
Sophie reports to Beth, her instructor.
"She closes her lips when I offer a drug
that makes her heart pump stronger."

"Chart data. You're not her doctor,"
says Beth. "Or daughter," Sophie replies.
"Celia watched the door for grandkids,
but now she doesn't care."

Celia's pigeon chest grows larger, her ribs
like pool rungs. She tells Sophie how
she perked coffee, made jokes and kringles
for Sölvig, her best friend from Lindstrom,
who may have died or forgotten her.

Celia dreams Sölvig's alto quavers:
From the deeps, Lord, bring us home.

The Mourning Dove

From naps, they wake in urine as aides crank open
windows from room to room. Aged patients wait
with goose bumps, mute, unwilling, and listen
near the half-drained pond beside the Walmart.

White throated sparrows seek *Sam Peabody, Peabody*
Peabody. The swamp sparrows' slurred liquid calls
fall through Pine Siskin's wheezy reeds.

"You'll see fine feathers in the Aviary," says Diane,
the nurse who wheels Helmer, Pam and Florence
to inhalers, eye drops, dinner or the milky Ensure.

The mourning dove coos, *ewe Ah ewe,* as the parakeet
pecks the crested pigeon, its wounded tonsure—Diane
dabs it with ointment on a Q tip. Well equipped, she
dispenses chocolate, Xanax, every sort of anodyne.

Maura Reminds Me

Of my mother. I can hardly
look when I must wash
between her useless legs.

"Wouldn't care to live
on someone else's schedule."
Mom's afraid of nursing homes.

Where I work, we pass inspection,
but we nurses feel ashamed each time
we pack a gaping ulcer
with neomycin and gauze.

Hips can't take the grating
of clean sheets. No matter how long
a grandma pads her hips, she sits
uneasy in this world. Mom says,
"I won't be a burden on my children."

Was the other way around for Maura—
her children kept on coming back
with laundry, till she fled here.

My mother is embarrassed.
"I puff just watching others work.
I'm shaky cracking eggs."

It's your turn, Ma, I say—
let other people do for you.

My lazy notions
don't set well with her,
and never will.

Maura's hair, like Mom's,
sticks straight up in back,
a cowlick where her head is flat.

Maura reaches for canning jars
while she sleeps. She watches
currants drip through muslin,
filling her cellar kettle
while the aide cranks her bed
up for the breakfast tray.

~

A brother and I told Mom
her home's with either one of us,
but how can I promise? I work.

Other brothers and sisters
don't mind Mom in care,
but they'd rather it was mine.

If they paid me, I told my husband.
Then I'd be her nurse at home.
It's him I lie to, and he knows it.

I'd sooner see our kids unschooled
than give her to someone else's daughter.

Mary Kate McNally Asks Me Every Day

"Why do you love me?"
"Because you are you," I always tell her.

"Not because I pay my bills on time?"
She grabs the nurse's station, standing
only to sign for her suite.
"Put the extras on my statement."
She says we have a fine hotel indeed.

"Why do you love me?"
She's like my Irish aunts,
a grammar snob, so I laugh
and say, "You speak with precision,
putting an audible comma before *which*.
You always say *to whom*."

"The rest all say *to who*, like owls!"
She chuckles at her joke. "Coming up
(she repeats for our pleasure) we girls
all read encyclopedias. Maude taught.
I made executive secretary,
meaning I ran the show.

"Why do you love me?" She twists
in her wheelchair to see me as I go.
Giving up, I turn her around,
so she can join the meds parade
from bed to bed as I administer

pills to the less fortunate— "elderly
gals in jogging pants," she says.

"I like your style," I say, "your
Blyley suit and purse." She softens
but asks, "Why do you *really* love me?"
"Because you're you, Mary Kate, a matriarch."
For her sons and her grandson, Young Doc,
who will diagnose her final air hunger;
and her daughter-in-law, who chose
to live across the street.

She couldn't drive them from her bed
with her sharp, fond tongue.

Robert and Mike, a Love Story

If you have to call it "Independent Living,"
you live on the edge of loss, so Robert said "pad."
They'd brought their king-size bed, the Waterford,
a leather bar and books. A TV so Mike could feed
his political needs with the News Hour, but Robert
turned it off when Mike got mad and tossed
his wine at the morons on screen.

With common walls thin, the prim married couple
other side, complained to the director: "*Why* do
Christian people have to stand—no decent way
to put it—homosexuals? The slender one's okay, but
the fat guy howls. Their bed sounds begin at night fall!"

Robert knew for months that Mike just wasn't right.
Then, offhand, the doctor said, "Dementia. Memory Care
is just a floor away." All Rob heard was Locked Ward,
too far away for them to be: "Together forty years!"
Younger at only sixty-eight, Rob fretted that Mike,
alone in a fearful rage—strapped down?—would die.

Then Schatzie Oster, a licensed practical nurse
with eyes as blue as truth and muscular legs—
a former farm wife—happened to evaluate
Mike at Happy Hour, so Robert offered
beer and wine. She asked if he had mints.
He did, so it was safe to sip one ounce of Bud.

Mike, seventy-six, napped, so Robert whispered
their story, and her eyes were soft and steady.
"Together you'll move to Assisted Living," she said.
"I'll make sure you don't have righteous neighbors."

Assisted alright, as long as Schatzie did it, but one P.M.
a registered nurse lost her cool when Mike spit his pill
and mooned her. Rob removed him to the bedroom.
Livid, the R.N. sputtered, "Alzheimer's—he should be
locked in. After another eval.—this time by me!"

"Not her," said the Charge Nurse, Schatzie's friend.
"Common sense doesn't come with a degree.
Michael's meds take time. They stay."

One calmer afternoon, Mike, who didn't recall
checkers, played dominos with Robert, and watched
Your Cheating Heart. By chance, Mike switched
to news, and Rob returned from the john to find
Mike glassy-eyed before the president he hated.

"Who's that?" Mike asked. How Robert missed
his lover's curses; he wept in the stiffest whiskey
and gave Mike watered wine, against the rules.
Then Schatzie came and offered her shoulder.

Melvin and Mary, Another Love Story

Melvin

In Assisted Living, I asked Schatzie,
our favorite nurse, to wheel my Mary
up from another floor, Skilled Care,
to lie with me each afternoon.

She lifted Mary into bed with me,
then closed the door. Never, with a wink
or look, did she remind us that we were old.
She didn't tell a soul, but then I broke my leg.

I exist in the room next to Mary's, farther
away from her than ever—we're never alone.
The doctor said, "You must adjust to aging
and loss of privacy."— "Easy for you to say,"
I said, "You're not sleeping in a single bed."

Shatzie

You'd think there was a law against love
for people over seventy! "A younger couple
has a double bed," I said to the director, who
replied that Melvin and Mary weren't married.

"So what," I said, "about their long life together?"
Our lawyer agreed, so the boss released the key
to the guest room (also used for death vigils).
Unbelievable—she gave them a leaflet on safe sex!

All eight children felt ashamed but the youngest.
"Let's not act like bastards. Common law's good
as church." The eldest said our chapel was better
and invited her parents to a wedding, their own.

Mary said they wouldn't— "Not until Robert,
our neighbor, can marry Mike." I say, Amen.

Schatzie's Party

At the Golden Oldies Jamboree,
the women sang six verses
of "Don't Fence Me In."

Little Audrey Jean, who's 93,
hadn't touched her pureed ham and peas.
"I'm clean dead!" she wailed.

So to check it out I felt her pulse.
"You're going like sixty," I told her.
"If you have a pulse, you can't be dead."

"Takes a while," she said,
"for a body to shut down."

"Why not eat to pass the time?" I said.
"Can't eat if I'm dead," she insisted.

"Does this look like heaven?" I asked.
"No, but everyone looks dead to me."

People get ideas—you can't change 'em,
so I changed the scene.

"Look lively," I told the other nurses.
"Serve ice cream!" I instructed the aides.

We called off the doctors, let the parrot out,
and brought in kids with therapeutic pets.

The dog ran in circles round the day room.
The cat went on a tear.

Audrey shrieked, “I’m dead!”
I didn’t hold her Haldol.

When Art raised his canes overhead, I said,
“Party’s over, let’s all go to bed.”

“I might be dead,
but I had fun,” said Audrey.

Nurses, You Strain to Lift

For Kate Dayton and Nancy Massman

Nurse Schatzie, wrestling death with both kind arms,
panicked—her frailest grandma tottered out the door
wearing only her robe in a blizzard. How Eleanor
didn't trip the exit alarm, no one knew for sure.
But she wasn't in the trunk room, closet, armoire,
or under the altar, where they'd found her the time before.

In came St. Clare, with bare shorn head, closed cape,
covered with snow, her habit of Umbrian brown on Ellie.
Clare barefoot as always, narrow as her bones.
St. Francis said, "*Buongiorno*, Mama Clara!" He'd heard
of her coming from the feathered monk, a blackbird.

Schatzie took Ellie, now lucid, to phone the sons she forgot
a decade past. Clare floated the stairs to her hospice workshop.
Vicky, Director of Nurses, arrived at the meeting sprayed
with Arpege. Schatzie followed, sneezing, with plates on a cart.
"Abbess Clare," Vicky said, "have some pizza, diet root beer."
Laughing, she added, "I'm starved as a shiftless Vo-Tech nurse!"

"You R.N.s clique," retorted Schatzie, "to dish the latest mess—
who's slow or can't do Medicare." Schatzie gossips too
but has no malice. She and her aides pad bed rails,
heat bedpans, smooth braces, fasten ankle bells,
and keep the fragile safe without restraints.

"Hear my rule for quarreling nuns," Clare said.
"Though nurses don't kneel like the lamb
Saint Francis trained to make us laugh,
Daughters, you strain to lift your heavy tasks,
the hours you strap upon your wrists. You run
from the sick to your pens and fear the state's
inspectors, who list your malpractice, forcing
this endless writing. I say no! Cardinals are hard
and overanxious, but I've refused their gold."

"Donna Vicky, let your nurses speak! Dispense
with grim portresses, grills, and double locks.
"We women have the power to change water
into wine, when we stay with souls
who need us for their journeys."

Clare sighed, pulled off her wimple,
took a pinch of ashes from her purse
to sprinkle on her silver hair.

"I'm the servant of my sisters.
I've consoled my nursing novices
with tears. I've kissed their feet.
In peace, these hospice nurses
escort the dying from this world."

"Go with swift pace,
unswerving light step—be messengers."

St. Francis Has a Picnic With St. Clare

Francis is dying to get out
of his flesh, like the sheath
upon the glass thermometer
I put beneath his tongue, so hot
his fever melts Celsius and Fahrenheit.

One final time, I long to bring him
to visit Clare but am afraid
he'd die on the way and then—
my Sister Ass is hauled
before the Board of Nursing.

St. Francis quits burning
for her sake and mine.
Clare waits outside her convent.
Her sisters set a trestle table
with bread, chianti, pesto.

As I push his wheelchair,
she places their feast
beneath a tree, where fire ants
consume their untouched meal.

"Pardon me, Abbess," I say, "Francis
can't sit straight, even with a bolster."
"Leave us—don't worry." She laughs
and points across the pond. I go.
Then I turn to gape at her slow rise.

Her bare soles clear the dandelions,
the rhododendrons and the linden trees.
The wheels of his chair begin
spinning him higher, facing her.
I wonder how she'll feed him
    hovering in air.
If angels brought manna? No.

Already full, these lovers
are impatient to be wholly still.

Sister Death and the Social Worker

For Deirdre Flesche; Mary and Dave Peterson

His *bleu celeste* eyes! I tell him every shift he shouldn't end
like this. At this home. "By my license, you'll get out," I swore.
And chuckling, he secured the trellis round the door,
where migrating pink-breasted grosbeaks bobbed like dahlias.

The others follow him. When all the leg alarms go off at once,
the nurse aides used to sprint, but now they wink. "It's Francis
with one of his field trips." The elders, puffing, wound
through Fellowship Park, bumping along the flagstone.
They sat on wooden benches, tossing their crutches, braces,
and canes to the golf-fine grass. Francis began to tell stories.

Peter (staphylococcus boils for twenty years) couldn't believe
that Francis kissed a leper. "Fucking missionaries," said Pete.
"Like guys against 'Nam, you brought the plague stateside
with your wussy, wimpy, peace protesting Agent-Orangers!"

"But our sister, the moon," said the friar, "wants peace,
not war. I was wrong when I was young and fought the Moors.
And a fool when I spent my youth carousing—French tunes,
cassoulet, crusty bread, cheese, Burgundy wine and women."

Peter's scrotum, like a biblical wine skin, was distended
and sore. He groaned, and Francis said, "Your heavenly body
will shed your pain." — "To hell with later!" Peter said.

As Peter eased his thighs on the patio lounger, wafted leaves
spun off the aspen in a sunset breeze. Francis waved them down,
and so did the women. "The sun's like camphor liniment," said Ellie.
Moving her arms with the others, she couldn't lift her fingers.
She grasped cones to keep her hands from turning into claws.

Their feathers glinting verdigris, the crows croaked ever lower, then
the motley flock sprang from the fence, releasing hacking caws
and grating rattles. Francis, a tenor with brio, sang harmony.

"I've ridden Brother Ass from Assisi to Mississippi,"
Francis sang. "Tell me about it," grumbled Evalina,
tossing popcorn she'd hoarded to the squirrels.

Tails behind the telephone wires,
carrion-loving ravens closed their beaks
as the saint started crooning Gregorian motets,
minus flats or sharps. "Ow! Don't touch,"
Ellie said, but she allowed Saint Francis
to stroke her locked and flaming feet.
"My pain is gone!" said Ellie,
"but Francis—are you okay?"

In blizzards of light, he faded,
the sound like flapping sheets.
"Whatever Doc has me on,"
said Peter, "it's too strong."

I'd seen it too—
Me, the professional
trained to record only facts.
Francis grew wings.
Transparent carmine feathers

lifted his shoulders.

As he blessed us, we knelt,
even those who couldn't
bend their knees.
I never could save anyone.

Sister Death!" he said.

Living Is to Suffer but Still Dance

For physical therapists of a certain age

In balmy water, warm as an infant's bath,
Suzy, once my patient, defies
fibromyalgia, swaying in the pool.

When it's time to go, she hoists
her booty up each step,
rolling out groans
and swear words,
as gravity takes back
her buttocks, hips and knees.

We swimmers, who suffer on land
from traveling inflammation,
empty the pool with our chorus of moans.
We limp to the sauna together.

Once a nun, our Suzy escaped
a prison, when Mother Superior
made her sing, *I'll be home*
for Christmas and *Smile*
though your heart is breaking
to prisoners on death row.

Zorba the Greek invited Suze
to live, take off her belt and dance.
So she boogied right out of her habit,
and she's been naked ever since.

Lyrics for my Bone Loss Blues

As we age...calcium flows out of our skeletons
into our tissues. –Atul Gawande, M.D.

Wood*peck*er who mistakes
a*lum*inum for wood our chimney for a tree—
his tattoo wakes me, it takes
turns with the radio's drumming beat, Art Blakey's.
The pecker calls E minor,
a one note repetition
he toots a sharp F higher—
  a note I seldom hear,
my stirrup calcified and anvil hammered to my ear.

Ain't no use in jivin' with Art.
Sing it! Sing it! Like Nina Simone.
Don't go losin'   those higher tones
to that bad-ass tinnitus!
Its dumb-dum   whine 'n'   thrumming.
A cranky aspirin side effect, but still
  I *take* that pill to *move* my body,
    shift my weight like Blakey,
 to the off-beat—
  weak joint.
It counts, but I blame my knee.

Cra*zy* red-head breaks his beak
to get me up, get out—

You lay-abed, it's time
to drill sunflower seed in loam—
soon up to my aching knuckles in
    potash and calcified lime.

I got the Bone Loss *Bluuues*!
    My poor synovial
    articulation,
    sin-syncopation,
    mineral migration—

Calcium spurts from marrow to line
    my arteries.
I creak and crunch in my own time.

Bathing Song for Villa

For all nurses' aides,
especially Poo Nam and Nimmi

From floor to floor, the nurses pound
mortars in pestles for the ancients—
grinding pills to keep their spirits
quiet, in the body longer.

Some elders do not want to live.
I see it in eyes when I wash faces.
How easily skin lifts, so the Bone Man,
double jointed, starts tap dancing.

The Spirit woman wears a nightgown
like water, smooth as a tear, but no tears
from elders on my far island, where mangoes grow.
Ancients slowly cure, sweet wrinkled like raisins.
Children shade them from the sun,
turn palm fronds East to West.

On this northern tundra, sexy mamas
in sweaters and blankets, freeze
a century and no one sees,
until she gets her picture in the paper.
"Anvilla Leary, born *1916*—
Villa's lived over 100 years!"

"Villa's lived too long," I tell this nurse.
Does she suppose a person whacks her arms

raising bruises, purple veins
on yellow plums, for nothing?
Villa needs the soft Pacific,
winter whirl pool.
With this Hoyer chair, I lower her
in the bath, where I soap her and sing.

Your belly—your children swam from it,
from you, their beginning—Bless it.
Bless your back curved over like bleached coral
with fish no longer swimming through.
Oh bless your bones.

THE GLORIFIED BODY

Pentecost

For Magda, who recalls the 1933 famine
and the Russian army outside Kiev in 1943

Far from Ukrainian buckwheat fields,
she gazes at bronzed-wing manikins
flying the cage from trough to beam.
"We foraged with corncrakes for grain,"
says Magda, called Baba, and she shrugs.

"Starving, we ate chaff and dust, then died
faster than cattle we slaughtered, us Kulaks."
A priest's peaked mitra above the burning field—
a breeze wafts incense over reeking wheat.

Her white head a perch for the Holy Ghost,
Baba Magda trails Christos on her sore feet
searching for the sparrows.

Amazing Grace

1.

How sweet the sound, whispers Joanie, as the organ
swells—Reverend Eddie playing Amazing Grace.
The doctor says, "he's better on the xylophone."
The Deaconess, scorned by Joan as a Lutheran nun,
sings a full chest tone, and Joanie envies her diapason.

"My rotten cigarettes!" she says. Her ex-, a drinker, fled
when Charlie, their only child, was ten; at just eighteen,
Charlie chose another family—men at war. Joan inhales
thinner air and sorrow. Caged, a parrot forgets to fly
before she'd deny her son. *Who saves a wretch like me...*

Him flying on the Persian Gulf, his plane a Predator.
Its missiles are called Hellfire. "I pray that he bails out."
I once was lost but now I'm found... Dead like the parrot?
Wearing rubber gloves, the nurse zip-locked and froze it.

2.

Safe—she prays that he will be. *Was blind but now I see..*
Whether it's her heart or lungs, how can she tell Charlie
she's dying? *Through many dangers, toils and snares…*
Joan's tears are leaking through her fingers, but Pastor
Eddie carries on despite her tremors.

May Charlie's whistle shrill on other Abu Ghraibs, she prays.
His plane land whole, unmortared. My homing pigeon, be a dove—
Don't bomb Babylon, other women's sons—destroy a vacant lot.
Or spiral high from fishing coves, away from little lives like ours.

No grandchildren, none. *I've already come...* "Are you in Mosul?"
'Twas grace that kept me safe... "Or did you just bomb Basrah?"
And mothers waiting for their sons upon this earth... *thus far.*
"I spanked you when I had to, tied your laces—now no mail."
And grace will lead me home. Grown, he flew to lose...

3.

To lose himself. "I'll know his face" *when we've been there*
*ten thousand years...*The large-print hymnal notes float up
and one by one, swim the blue to wires where they perch
like robins. *Bright shining as the sun...* She's hoping he isn't
one of heaven's choristers, singing the bass line of her death.
We've no more days... Her flattened EKG—not yet.

To Sing God's praise... Fix my heart, the organ's wheezing.
"God, remove my bitterness, self-pity," Joan rebukes herself.
Not waiting, Jesus' mother trailed after him in poverty.
Birds of air have nests, the sons of women no cover
but rain, no address but the one the wind blows.

For Charlie's head a helmet made of straw.
"Son," she breathes, "go on.... *As when*
we'd first begun." Singing, she goes over.

Mother Helena Rises Up

I'm forced to die in this Protestant home,
last nun of Basil's Athanasian order, but I'm
stronger, at ninety-nine years, than this priest
who totters with the host in its holy pix. Viaticum,
final sacrament I'd rather steal from the chapel.

Like saintly Gorgonia. Her tumor drove her
to the altar she used as her hospital bed.
Rubbing the sacred bread on her wasted limbs,
she resurrected herself before the glorified
body, whole and pink. No miracle for me.

I'm dragged, like young Gorgonia by teams
of mules who push us into bed and pull us out.
To my Maker—make it *Her*—I pray to Sophia
for blessed death, a cure from shining hooves.

~

Sophia's good demise, a cure for hooves!
To the Father—no, *Mother*—bless our mules
who mean to help and push our chairs, and bind
our wounds too tight. We're nagged like Gorgonia
by wholesome bodies. None as sere as mine.
No miracle for me, a living mummy, my flesh
unresurrected, glory died. Gorgonia rubbed
the wafer on her wasted limbs with fear
that God would be hospitable, invite her up.

I prefer to steel myself against the altar, older
than my strength, my beads, Viaticum I eat
upon the road at ninety-nine. Bury this tottering
Athanasian Basil boy, this priest, his Godly pix.
I'll live a nun in this Protestant place, the last!

Question the Abuser, Who is God

The aging women, Room 110
yelled loud and hard at 2 a.m.
Nurse and aides ran down the hall,
but couldn't quiet them at all.

Eve stumped her crutches to the door,
and cried, "I won't sleep in hell no more."
"Ghosts," said Rose, "take over the floor."
She didn't make much sense at all.

Judith could not get out of bed.
Her feet were higher than her head.
Her speech was gone—aphasic dread.
We couldn't comfort her at all.

Her feeble roommates couldn't crank
her bed—so who contrived this prank,
making Judy faint and anxious.
Why must she suffer through it all?

Why does Eve weep for her father?
Why does Rose rage at her brother?
Why the broken time, mad pother?
Mind out of mind—that defeats us all.

Now the dressings, then syringe,
next the night sweats, oxygen,
final suctioning, lung's whinge.
Poltergeists of pain, and that is all.

She Sees the Future in the Past

She admires the honesty of starlings
drawing on the autumn sky
with a million murmuring wings!
Beginning easy, a cigar-shape

drawing on the autumn sky,
a zeppelin equipped with hatches.
Beginning easy, a cigar-shape
for escape—a whoosh, whoosh

zeppelin equipped with hatches
sounds like the extra-clean cycle to her.
For escape—a whoosh, whoosh.
Starlings fold the edge of a sheet of birds,

sounding like the extra-clean cycle to her,
but more menacing—a roar of hurricanes.
Starlings fold the edge of a sheet of birds.
Winds strain, dragging this murmuration—

but more menacing—a roar of hurricanes
in the western seas, derechos east.
Winds strain, dragging this murmuration
of starlings to the melting poles.

Roars in the western seas, derechos east—
Starlings drawing on the autumn sky
are beginning easy, a cigar-shape
ending with a mushroom cloud.

Hannah's Sermon

1.

It was evening, it was morning, the first day.
I thank God he didn't make me a man
when I see these pitiful specimens slurping
coffee—No benschen on bliss! I mustn't kvetch.
Give them to their kids to feed, I advised
the dietician, but offer not pearls to putzers,
those who deal in Brussels sprouts or onions.
When I was only five, my mama gave me
honey cakes for school, so I would learn.
At Shalom Home the study groups but here
the hymn-alongs. No matter. With Sarah near—
she swears by my challah, my recipes—I snooze
quite well with one big ear stuck out above
my Minnesota comforter, awaiting the Messiah.

Minnesota comfort is too late for the Messiah.
I sleep better without those Purim fire works
in my ears, but good old Hannah warbling hymns!
No benschen on bliss. I kvetch and Sarah fears
I'm missing Shalom Home, but let them
study the honey cake recipe. I cried from love,
the hardest school, and onions Mama put upon
my chest. I tell the putzer doctors—a poultice
for a cough. Coffee shouldn't blister men.
Let their daughters make them challah
to dip—then it's not too hot. Offer not pearls
to those who kill the cabbage. I thank God

he didn't make me a man when I began
this evening, all those mornings, the first day.

2.

If I said all there was to say about my life
while standing on one foot, I wouldn't have
sugar diabetes. No matter how short your wife,
lean over and take her advice, as my Aaron quoted
some Torah sage. Or Hillel? In the chapel no one
listens as aides roll us in and out. So stop! I yell.
I make the nurse guess this riddle: Born into

the world with clenched fists, we leave open
handed—why? She shakes her head and pops
a pill on my tongue, and shoots my shot. "Because
we exit life with nothing," I say. "But your daughter,"
the nurse says, "loves you!" Love won't pack a donkey
for the dark road, and my daughter's children won't
ride behind her when she travels life in a single day.

3.

Behind me, my daughter is riding her days with me,
but the grandkids aren't toting our black luggage.
—"How they love you!" —"Love won't pack
my donkey with nothing," I say. Cross my heart.
The nurse shoots me, stops my tongue with a pill.
With prying fingers, I open and close her fists.

Why? The nurse can't get this riddle: 'We're born
to bliss, so why do you wheel us out?' So stop and listen—
Pastor preaches the wisdom of a Torah sage, in chapel
where I lie back with diabetes and my own advice.

As Aaron misquoted Hillel—no matter how smart
your wife is, bow to her while standing on one foot.
I wouldn't have high sugar or this fuss, if I'd said
all there was to say about my life.

Just to See Him Smile

Al Locksley adores Betty Grable,
her endless legs in black-seamed hose
decked his bunk off Coral Sea. He pays
decades later at Veteran's. The doctor
says it was those chippies. Al *don't know*
how he *drive a gov'ment wheel chair,*
turning toward Pokeeno. The slow
syphilis makes mind-holes. He smiles.

Time for insulin, pills? he asks
again and forgets the answer.
Betty's bosom—*what happens next?*—
always round. The calendar is
baseball, or *the Christmas boy choir*!
The hour is *what's to eat*? He'll find
the nurse he loves, show her the door-
prize he won for her. He smiles.

Pastor Ed tells Al to sing out strong
around the player piano. Al lifts
his thighs, just stumps, in time
to the beat—*Oh Rock of Ages*!
The year is always '45. Al begs,
more Spam now! He loses his soup
all over the loud purple neck tie
we gave him, just to see him smile.

With one skipped heartbeat, *Is it time*?
He loses his schedule, and at the end,
tells the night aide, *I'm dying* and does.
And he had such a wonderful smile.

Bill's Last Day With the Railroad

He woke as doors along the corridor swung
free with clicking shudders, and views
from windows changed like slides—one city,
state, another; one year, another. First stop he's ten
when he jumps off at Jake's for angling.

Next he's sixty at his brother's funeral,
the pallbearers moving slow as freight cars shunted
to a side track in Chicago, '45. Bill and the boys
are demobilized. Called back, his job's been saved!

His bathrobe's askew over his navy jacket—Can't be
late! Great Northern says to drop his other job, his wife,
kids, and life to be on time! The waitress shouldn't tease—
the engineer? *Zantac, Bill?* No, he's the working stiff who oils
the wheels, steel axles. *Vanilla shake, Bill?* He pounds his locker.

Clickety-clack on rails makes him shout: *I'll never have another.
Had no whiskey for fifty years!* Legs shaky over tracks on gravel,
he avoids the men in white who write in black—traveling inspectors.
We can handle dawn in great Des Moines. Then tickets please!

As the caboose crew chows down, the joyride's for Bill;
fifteen, he shivers on Milwaukee Road rails in a box car from St. Paul.
The crew, used to catching stows, laughs him back to school—
Can't shave peach fuzz. In three years, he's back and grown
to 5 foot 5—eight inches over standard gauge.

In five years he makes brakeman. *Bill, be still for heaven's sake!*
Down Rock Island Pacific corridors, he leaps the couplings, fishplate.
Going slow round a curve, Union Pacific grading steep, when an agent
from Missoula teletypes a slide. Loco takes ten miles to stop, cross-tie
sleepers holding, though rails are buried up ahead. He lurches left—

Let me go! he says, as the diesel pulls him right. The brass destroyed
his way of life with Amtrak; still the Bad Lands—like a deck of cards—
whip by the track, buttes then ridges flipping up, fast deals the wind blew
four hands; now, clutching his arms—*Please, your legs in your pajamas!*
Rain on those new dome cars—not the real thing—he'd staked
his future on his pension. *Time for bed!* Steel whines on creosoted timbers.

Their golden wedding trip in Pullman bunks, a train-man's holiday
shaking, like fast jazz—*the Atchison, Topeka and the Santa Fe,*
the City of New Orleans, its boogie woogie blues. Then Lincoln,
Denver and Boise. *What Bill, you're still up? Your teeth go in this cup.*
Countless burg-mounds: Oshkosh, Winston, and Buck. *A lozenge
to help you doze?* No! He hears the whistle blow dark tunnels.

Across Menasha, Fond du lac, Prentice—never-beens, backwater
milk runs. *What's a matter?* Bill heads for the exit: *Don't stop me!*
Between the rails and street are fifty years, a gold tie pin and coach pass.
Alarm bells sound, signal lights red, crossing bars down,
a fog upon the tracks, the warming noise.

Saga of the Lake Cabin in the '80s

His '50's story: our dad promises, "a lake house,
Bluebell!" After five hours in the car, mom
whacks high grass to the door, weeping in anger,
"seven kids, three in diapers, and an out-house!"

The old foundation sags but rises
on in-laws wedging pavers.
The roof burgeons with moss and uncles
shaving dry rot off the crossbeams.

Grandpa puffs his Muriel cigar,
pulls the motor's cord—putt puff putt
puff—bang! He rows to the brush pile
and baits his hook with a fat black leech.

Gram can't catch her breath to swing
the scythe more than twice.
Instead she hangs our clothes
from the balsam tree to the pier pole.

The boards of the dock,
like piano keys, go down
and up beneath our feet
until one cracks—

the pier breaks into planks,
and Grandma trudges past in the water,
her sheets full of wind.
When I run to help, she yells "no thanks!"

Gram laughs—"I'm grand!
Quick season the cast iron pan,
and start the charcoal grill." Flames
lick their reflections in the lake.

Great aunt stirs Welsh rarebit as Grandpa
climbs the hill, his pail full of walleyes.
Our aunt fears choking, so he fillets
white flesh from Y-shaped bones.

Window glass reflects the gallimaufry
of outside/inside—wet laundry hanging
on the rope Gram strings from rafters.
The way thunder startles us—

Especially Great uncle playing Rummy,
and Gramp drinking his martini—
he ruminates his storm thoughts,
like laundry, dark from light.

But it all runs together, making
our communal load a pearly gray.
For the family reunion, where we
middle aged children strain gravy.

We're never done setting the table
with daisies, hushing the kids, the oldsters—
their arguments and beer, a cousin
stalking off for Solitaire.

When the food is ready, the cook deplores
a rolling bulge above the stove—raccoons
in the attic! He wedges a plywood board
on the ceiling above three push brooms.

Raccoons rock and roll but don't fall through.
Coyotes wail like grieving banshees. The Grands
disappear into mists of sleep; before dawn,
Grandma startles awake, despite her oxygen.

Uncles fasten the pier planks twice over,
like the laundry. The boards depress
and rise beneath many feet,
all dancing to the music of this ruin.

My Father Contemplates His Days

Hunching beneath twenty pounds
of pumpkin seeds, he whistles
through his nose. I lug
his forty pounds of thistle mix.

Strung pie pans make a tinny racket
to rid his feeders of grackles and jays.
On the Horicon Marsh, he frees
the squirrels he nicked then caged.

He shoots a cat with his B-B gun—it yowls
and misses a flapping osprey,
which tucks its neck and sails above
the tourist boat, nearing the rookery.

Kite-shaped swans hang, not falling,
beneath the tamaracks. My father opens
his folding chair and sits to fish
as black-crested herons descend.

He casts away from them,
in the deepest part of the pool.

The Eagle

The spring he is 80, Father calls on Claire
to fish Columbus lake, where the eagles
tease muskellunge and snatch bass. On shore,
rapid chip-like calls make squirrels tremble—
eagles warning anglers to keep off the walleyes.

Grandpa's by-pass heart — I'm scared; I'd tried
to teach Claire how to run the motor, but she's small.
If he were stricken, she couldn't pull the cord.
A skill I knew at her age, fourteen. Her life jacket
discarded, she sits on a floatable cushion waving

while her guide lowers his Mayville golf cap
on his eyes then steers them well past the rings
the sandbar makes in fish scale water— high
an eagle soars on flattened wings into the sky.

The Family Recessional Recorded

Visiting dear survivors, we're reluctant
to learn how much the self goes into hiding.
Even before first eulogies, funeral hymns haunt
our elders, even us—cousins in the middle.

The body recedes part by part.
Our German uncles' big hearts will skip and slow
because of bigger bellies—liverwurst and stollen.
Some Irish aunts—not Ruth, who tamped tobacco
down in biddies' white clay pipes at wakes—
cannot draw breath to get the air they lost,
when hooked on cigarettes.

For Aunt Hilaire, I taped our children's voices,
asking only for her memories on the other side.
Thanks! (in her brown and micrographic script)
I love Claire's nursery rhymes and Matthew's story.
As a lady who ignored all lapses in decorum, she
didn't fill my fifteen minutes with her eighty years.

Now old enough, I'd say—let history take care of itself.
But where is my tape of Zurich bells above our baby's
rocking cradle, each chime conducting him to sleep.
Bells, ranged high and low, reverberate, tail off
to merge with the Limat River's susurrations.
Each note, rich or thin, is carried on seed-wafting air,
only to begin again, again. Again, Frau Münster's
tintinnabulations, unerased, still ring wherever we are.

My brother Tom, his video camera whirring at our parents,
was preserving our progenitors, making a family record.
Resigned, Dad and Mom paused before full plates, bratwurst,
sauerkraut and chips. They waited on hard benches to eat,
while Tom recorded the bloom-bronzed Rock River's weeds
and plied them with historical soft questions.

When Tom spliced this scene into his longer saga, he didn't
mean to erase our parents' answers. He had the bridge
behind Grandma, who opens her mouth to speak;
then a grandchild dances by the bandstand.
Trumpets blare, drums tattoo, and fiddles begin to waltz.
Emily keeps dancing till her father's film runs out.

We Wait in the Night With Mary

My mother's voice, sibilant, rises on *Mary,*
full of grace, and the moist white noise—
her machine condensing oxygen,
what she needs to live, from ordinary air
I breathe so easily. Comforted, she hears
and feels her warm breath making words.
From the sleeping loft, I breathe with her.

Rosary beads click, glowing in the dark, as large
as her knotted split knuckles. Her fingers count five
decades in a day. Each week of her life, she travels
with fifteen mysteries—five joyful, five sorrowful,
and five glorious. I remember three. Keeping awake,
she prays till she completes Our Father, Hail Mary—
Blessed art thou among women—her last Glory Be.

Before she prays, she reads of betrayals, murders
solved by Mrs. Marple, Father Brown, or Hercule Poirot.
Detectives must have denouements. Rosaries are round,
so she comes again to angels and His sharp star—Stumbles,
whips and pounded nails should never happen. But they do.
She counts on His resurrection, but the sorrowing loop
continues with *Blessed is the fruit of thy womb,*

Jesus. She wakes at two, beads hooked on thumbs.
She's had it with circular journeys, so she prays
for her sons, one lost to death, one estranged.
Awake with my own absences, two the same,
I try to say *Holy Mary, pray for us.* I join

the queue I was born in and could exit
but do not, and neither do my brothers.

Not from the cloud her breath makes,
the long line of her chant.

She Remembers to Inspire

For Gwen playing Chopin

Playing, she forgets to breathe.
She says it's not her fingers
releasing each measure whole,
but the singer inside her.

'Inhale,' she writes at every bar,
and holds her slow inhalation,
suspending plateaus, the slopes
of notes, her life beyond cancer.

~

I begin to climb the hill, retaining
my oxygen for two long strides.
Pursing my lips, I exhale
the way my mother expelled
air trapped in her lungs' alveoli.

Wondering how much time I have,
I practice for emphysema.
May I go on despite my smoking,
lungs clear these thirty years.

~

Mute singer holding your breath
to span fatigue and chemotherapy,

play the white keys and the black
half-steps in between.

~

I keep on climbing
despite discordant notes,
the rasps of my breath,
unsteady steps.

With greedy lungs,
I'm breathing in and singing out
until the woman playing rests her hands.

His Mooring

The time before the last he lowers anchor
from his wooden rowboat in the lake,
mackerel clouds unroll above a sandbar.

He's drifting from the outlet, from the shore.
Gulls are beaking minnows in his wake,
the time before the last he lowers anchor.

When the sun cracks like an egg, he's gone too far:
light shining through fine china, then it breaks.
Mackerel clouds unroll above a sandbar.

His life jacket buoys him—he's no swimmer.
Winds pushing icy breakers make him ache
the time before the last he lowers anchor.

Though he never made a cast, he smells nearby
the perch his wife is sizzling with the bacon.
Mackerel clouds unroll above a sandbar.

He's tethered, but his boat is left unmoored.
He can't even swallow for her sake.
The time before the last he sets his anchor
as mackerel clouds unroll above a sandbar.

Genius at Home in the Universe

After lines from Gitanjoli by Rabindranath Tagore

Einstein pulls a goofy face, his tongue thrust out
to mock the ones who grab his frowsy coattails.

As they stroll by the Rhine, the cat on his shoulder
plays with the smoke from his Meerschaum pipe.

Albert's friend, Tagore, who lags behind laughing,
rewrites Albert's theories to the speed of—*ah, the light dances.*

While they're sailing Lake Constance, *lilies and jasmine*
surge up on the crest of the waves of light!

They forget to tack in a gale-driven swell
or trim the canvas wings across the catboat's prow.

One high breaking comber—the craft heels and founders
Clinging to hull, cat clawing his hair,

Albert tells Rabi, to rest in the surf, assured—
"our bodies are in transit on the energy of stars!"

The Glorified Body

1.

An old woman's death is far below
frontiers, where pain is peaked
so high it might reverse
as nerves are numbed,
the newborn's head pressing on
pelvic bones, then out—

"A bloody show," they said,
"the head is crowning!"

There's something to show
for childbirth, but what of this
straining of the body out
beyond the body?

"Though I'm sick at eighty-eight,"
she said, post incision,
half her stomach gone,
"in God's eye, I'm just a baby."

She looks forward to her new body.
Her second coming together
will be successful, not like this

dying from the inside out,
ending in the rotten sweet
smell of cancer, antimatter
on clavicle and femur.

Lovely long bones cradle short bones,
tent poles for the trying
flesh—consumed but multiplied.

See the adult's blue temples,
the open skull beneath
an infant's scalp
drawn tight like doe skin on a drum.

Pulse beating, liquid eyes
held by the thinnest membranes.

2.

Only an observer could
think of pain as a tunnel.

Does a tumor flower?
Can a dying person learn
to love her death?

3.

The curve of cheek into jaw,
eyes gravely set among the small
orbital bones—

All reassemble
in the final moments
we hope.

Will our souls,
like yeast,
leaven dough
to multiply,
a ferment,
and this time
no kneading,
no bearing down?

A finger lifted from dough
makes a hollow,
but rising fills it in.

When we rise,
will fingers from past lives
leave shining prints,
or will our new bodies erase
memory, all our flesh-fine meetings?

Here we meet, our skin on skin
but then, in the glorified body,
will we penetrate or linger,
rainbows canceling each other,
becoming clear white light?

Never dark or lonely,
will our colors leach as we
lose ourselves in God's holy ether?

It's enough to make you sick
of ecstasy, nostalgic
for the birth-marked body,
which must be fed.

4.

"Have you anything here to eat?"
Jesus came from death to ask for breakfast.

The disciples, mouths gaping,
followed his every bite—
broiled sturgeon, raw honey.

"Touch me and see
a spirit doesn't have
flesh and bones like mine."

What sort of body is this?
Not a ventriloquist's
dummy for the soul.
His body is his voice,
music in every cell.

His hands are solid as bread
with its honeycombed holes.

Impossible—he is
a wave, a particle.
He feeds the fire,
turns the fish.

Hurtling through space,
his body is still here. With us. We're slow.

We used to think
if we knew where we were
we'd never know for sure how fast we're going.

Even the glorified
body is not what we think.

Gift

In memory of my father

In a flurry they descend, as if the sky
has feathers. Claws first, white breasts,
peach throats, and he counts them—five.

They choose his feeder though it's empty.
He doesn't have the strength to fill it up,
but these are plump and need no more.

No contentious grackles chase the bluebirds
from nothing or, making their own drab luck,
scrounge hulls the squirrels spit out.

Still these five, much bluer than cerulean
crayons, than a grand-child's painting.
He has only to gaze—they stay.

Advance Praise

The Music of this Ruin has a delicious sense of discovery and tenderness, as well as humor. Pat Barone gives us powerfully crafted portraits of elders who are being looked after and I dare say loved by the narrator in the poems. The poet's voice is a nurse whose keen eye, wit and wisdom dignify those who are losing or have lost command of their bodies, memories, and situations. The arc of the book becomes ever more intimate as it explores the life and death of the narrator's older parents. The role of birds in these poems will delight readers, including caged birds in care facilities that the elders watch and protect and free flying bluebirds that are a gift to a dying man.

~Margaret Hasse, poet of recent books, *Between Us* and *Shelter*

The poems on the old people in the nursing home is quite a fine piece of work. Like all good poetry, what is suggested is what is most powerful. After reading them I could feel the pent-up life of the old ladies in the midst of kindness and good care. At that stage it nearly scared me.

~Patrick C. Power, author of *Once a Brother, Book of Irish Curses,* and other works

THE AUTHOR

Patricia Barone publishes her fifth book with Taj Mahal Press. Her most recent poetry book, *Your Funny, Funny Face,* was published by Blue Light Press. A previous collection, *The Scent of Water,* is from the same press. New Rivers Press published her first book of poetry, *Handmade Paper*, and a novella, *The Wind*. Her short stories have been published by Wising Up Press, Peter Lang, Prentice/Merrill, Plume/ Penguin, American Writing and West Wind Review. She has received a Loft-McKnight Award of Distinction in poetry, a Lake Superior Contemporary Writers Award for a short story, and a Minnesota State Arts Board Career Opportunity Grant for a workshop with the Irish poet, Eavan Boland.

www.ingramcontent.com/pod-product-compliance
Lightning Source LLC
Chambersburg PA
CBHW022159160726
48282CB00024B/256
9788182537248